Marcus Aurelius (121–180 CE) was a Roman emperor and Stoic philosopher renowned for his wisdom, integrity and dedication to virtue. As one of the last "Five Good Emperors", he governed during a time of political and military challenges, demonstrating remarkable leadership and resilience. His private writings, later compiled as *Meditations*, reveal a deeply reflective mind striving to live ethically and thoughtfully. Revered as one of history's great thinkers, Aurelius's philosophy emphasizes self-discipline, mindfulness and living in harmony with nature, offering timeless guidance for those seeking clarity and purpose in life.

Gill Hasson has 20 years' experience teaching and writing on a range of issues to do with personal and professional development, mental health and wellbeing. She is the author of more than 22 books; the bestselling *Mindfulness, Mindfulness Pocketbook, Emotional Intelligence, Positive Thinking,* the *Sunday Times* bestseller *How to Deal with Difficult People*, plus other books on the subjects of resilience, communication skills and assertiveness.

MEDITATIONS

MEDITATIONS

Timeless Wisdom Distilled

MARCUS AURELIUS

Edited by Gill Hasson

JOHN MURRAY

ONE

First published in Great Britain by John Murray One in 2025
An imprint of John Murray Press

SRD

Editor copyright © Gill Hasson 2025

The material for *Meditations* is based on *The Thoughts of the Emperor M.
Aurelius Antonius*, translated by George Long, published by Bell & Daldy,
London 1862, and is now in the public domain. This edition is not sponsored or
endorsed by, or otherwise affiliated with George Long, his family or heirs.

A CIP catalogue record for this title is available from the British Library

Hardback ISBN 978 1 399 82148 3
ebook ISBN 978 1 399 82149 0

Typeset by KnowledgeWorks Global Ltd.

Printed and bound in India by Manipal Technologies Limited, Manipal

John Murray Press policy is to use papers that are natural, renewable and
recyclable products and made from wood grown in sustainable forests.
The logging and manufacturing processes are expected to conform to
the environmental regulations of the country of origin.

John Murray Press
Carmelite House
50 Victoria Embankment
London EC4Y 0DZ

John Murray Press
123 S. Broad St., Ste 2750
Philadelphia, PA 19109

www.johnmurraypress.co.uk

John Murray Press, part of Hodder & Stoughton Limited
An Hachette UK company

MIX
Paper | Supporting
responsible forestry
FSC™ C104740

Contents

Contents

Preface

THE COLLECTION OF thoughts and ideas in *Meditations* comes from the personal journals of Marcus Aurelius (121–80 CE) during the years he was Roman emperor – from 161 to 180 CE.

He set down his musings, observations and thoughts on the Stoic approach to life simply for his own benefit – to help him think, act and live well. Centuries later, his writings were organized for publication into 12 books with numbered sections to refer to individual "meditations".

Marcus's collection of personal writings offers insights into Stoicism, an ancient Greek school of philosophy aimed at helping people to be virtuous and to understand the world – how to relate to it and how to best live in it.

Stoicism teaches that virtue – being a good person – means living in harmony with the divine Reason (also referred to as God, Providence or the Universe) that governs nature and to accept with equanimity changes of circumstances or fortune, particularly any that are unpleasant.

A fundamental principle of Stoicism is the distinction between what is within our control and what is outside of our control. Stoics believed that, while we cannot control events – what happens to us – we *can* control how we respond to them: with courage, wisdom, temperance and justice.

The Stoics' belief system did not revolve around a personal God. Instead, the Stoics took a pantheistic view, meaning that God is synonymous with nature or the universe itself; that God is not a person, but exists in everything and everyone. God is everything, and everything is God.

It was within the framework of Stoicism that Marcus strove to live his life. He searched for answers to metaphysical questions – questions about the nature of reality and existence: What is my purpose? How can I manage misfortune, difficulties and challenges? How do I live with the knowledge that someday I will no longer exist?

He also posed ethical questions: How can I be a good person and ensure that what I do is right?

Nearly two thousand years later, Marcus's aphorisms – astute observations, thoughts and ideas embodying general truths – continue to offer insights and practical advice for our lives today. They encourage us to reflect on our actions and beliefs and so better navigate life's challenges and find contentment and inner peace.

Throughout the *Meditations* – of which there are nearly 500, varying in length from one sentence to long paragraphs – Marcus returns to the same core themes and issues such as how to be authentic, interact with other people, live in harmony with nature, accept what cannot be controlled, cope with change, and come to terms with death and the brevity of life.

This book – *Meditations: Timeless Wisdom Distilled* by Marcus Aurelius – includes 101 of his meditations and covers all the key themes that are part of Stoic philosophy. The arrangement of the meditations follows the traditional division into books, which seem to follow a chronological order according to when and where Marcus wrote them.

With the exception of the introductory Book One, on each left-hand page you will find one of Marcus's thoughts or ideas, as translated from the original Greek text by the English Classical scholar George Long in 1862 and published under the title *The Thoughts of the Emperor M. Aurelius Antoninus.**

On each facing page you will read a brief explanation of the meditation, with advice on how you can reflect on it in a way that is relevant to our lives today.

While Marcus's meditations might not have all the answers, they still have resonance – almost two thousand years after they were written.

---

* George Long, *The Thoughts of the Emperor M. Aurelius Antoninus* (London: Bell & Daldy, 1862). Long's translation has sometimes been modernized for the sake of clarity.

BOOK ONE

BOOK ONE

BOOK ONE OF *Meditations* consists of Marcus Aurelius acknowledging and thanking the people who have had a positive influence on his life, with a focus on those who instilled in him the values characteristic of a good Stoic. His acknowledgements are a good introduction to the book's themes.

In 1.3, for example, Marcus acknowledges that from his mother he learned "abstinence, not only from evil deeds, but even from evil thoughts; and further, simplicity in my way of living, far removed from the habits of the rich".

In a number of the meditations in Book One, he expresses his gratitude to his teachers, who taught him, for example, "not to meddle with other people's affairs, and not to be ready to listen to slander" (1.5). He writes that, from his teacher Rusticus, he had learned to forgive others who sought forgiveness (1.7); from his teacher Apollonius, that a person can stand firm but also remain flexible (1.8); and, from Sextus, to live in harmony with nature (1.9).

Friendship was important to Aurelius – he states that he has learned how to receive good deeds from friends without either being overly thankful or showing ingratitude by failing to thank them (1.8); "to look carefully after the interests of friends, and to tolerate ignorant persons, and those who form opinions without consideration" (1.9); "not to be indifferent when a friend finds fault, even if he should find fault without reason, but to try to restore him to his usual disposition" (1.13); and "to believe that I am loved by my friends" (1.14).

Marcus also writes that he has learned "not frequently nor without necessity to say to anyone, or to write in a letter, that I have no leisure; nor continually to excuse the neglect of duties required by our relation to those with whom we live, by alleging urgent occupations" – in other words, not to be too busy to spend time with people who are important to him.

Marcus recognized the importance of "equal rights and equal freedom of speech" and of "a government which respects most of all the freedom of the governed". He credits his uncle, adoptive father and predecessor, Emperor Antoninus Pius, with having taught him many things that would be important to his role as emperor. This includes the observation in 1.16 not to seek popular approval, to be firm and fair, and to listen to those who propose something that would benefit others.

Finally, in 1.17 Marcus Aurelius shows his gratitude for having good people in his life: "To the gods I am indebted for having good grandfathers, good parents, a good sister, good teachers, good associates, good kinsmen and friends, nearly everything good."

BOOK TWO

2.8

" Through not observing what is
in the mind of another a man has
seldom been seen to be unhappy;
but those who do not observe the
movements of their own minds
must of necessity be unhappy. "

NOT KNOWING WHAT others think of you will rarely make you unhappy, but failure to know your own mind always will.

Self-esteem – your estimation of your worth – comes from two sources: what others think of you and what you think of yourself. Certainly, much of our happiness is dependent on what we think of how others perceive us. But being overly concerned about what other people think of you takes up time and energy, leaving you feeling insecure and anxious.

If you wouldn't invite someone into your house, don't let them into your head.

Instead, be aware of your own mind. If you know what's important to you – your values and beliefs – you will stand firm; you will feel confident and content.

2.11

" Since it is possible that you may depart from life this very moment, regulate every act and thought accordingly. "

WHAT WOULD BE important to you if tomorrow were your last day? If you were to live one day as if it were your last, what worries and concerns would you let go of? Your mistakes? Your to-do list? What you do or don't own? Your social media profile? Other people's approval?

What really matters to you? Spend more time and thought on what's important to you and less time on the inconsequential. Living as if each day is your last doesn't mean that nothing else matters at all – the washing up still needs to be done, the bills still need to be paid, you still need to brush your teeth.

You can't take a "last day approach" all the time, but every now and again it can remind you to put things in perspective.

2.11 (continued)

❝ But death certainly, and life,
honour and dishonour, pain
and pleasure – all these things
equally happen to good men
and bad, being things which
make us neither better

nor worse. ❞

===

LIFE AND DEATH, glory and shame, pain and pleasure, all of these happen to the good people and the bad. So do joy and despair, wealth and poverty.

Even when harmful things happen, they don't have to harm your good character.

Good things happen to us. Bad things happen to us. Things go right, things go wrong. The bad guys often win, the good guys often lose.

So why bother being one of the good guys if the rewards are so uncertain?

Because, although the rewards of doing good might be outside your control, deserving them is not. Deserving success is up to you, getting it not necessarily so. So, aim to be one of the good guys. Will you always be appreciated or rewarded? No. Will it be worth it? Yes. Because it's the right way to live.

2.14

" For the present is the only thing
of which a man can be deprived,
if it is true that this is the only thing
which he has, and that a man cannot
lose a thing if he has it not. "

THE PAST HAS happened; it can't be taken away from you. The future hasn't happened; there's nothing yet to be taken away.

You can't lose the past or the future; if you haven't got something, how can anyone take it away from you? What you do have is the present – it is yours to do with what you will.

2.15

" Remember that all is opinion. "

- Dogs are superior to cats.

- Pelé was the greatest ever footballer.

- Dark chocolate is better than milk chocolate.

- Living in the country is more pleasant than living in a city.

- The monarchy should be abolished.

These are not facts but opinions – subjective personal views, judgements or beliefs. No one thing is inherently better than the other.

The ability to accept opinions and perspectives that are different from your own allows you to feel at ease with a diverse range of people – people of different ages, backgrounds and experiences. Rather than try to change other people's beliefs and opinions, seek to understand them.

Today, think of an opinion or belief that you know to be different from yours. Find out more – why might a person have that opinion? Be kind – give them the benefit of the doubt.

2.15 (continued)

" And manifest too is the use of
what was said, if a man receives
what may be got out of it as far
as it is true. "

IT'S ALSO THE case that, as far as there is truth in what someone says, you can benefit from another person's beliefs and opinions.

BOOK THREE

3.1

" And again, figs, when they are
quite ripe, gape open; and in the
ripe olives the very circumstance of
their being near to rottenness adds
a peculiar beauty to the fruit. And
the ears of corn bending down,
and the lion's eyebrows, and the
foam which flows from the mouth
of wild boars, and many other
things – though they are far from
being beautiful, if a man should
examine them severally – still,
because they are consequent upon
the things which are formed by
nature, help to adorn them, and
they please the mind. "

EVERYTHING IS BEAUTIFUL, in its own way.

If it's a natural process – a consequence of nature – it's as beautiful as its original source.

3.3

" You have embarked, you have
made the voyage, you are come
to shore; get out. "

In the context of the rest of this meditation, Marcus Aurelius seems to be saying here: "You were born, you have lived and now you are at the end of your life. It's over."

Another interpretation might be: wherever your journey has brought you, get out and make the most of it.

3.5

" Let the deity which is in you be
the guardian of a living being. „

LET YOUR CONSCIENCE be your guide.

Trust your values and moral principles and make decisions that align with them.

If you have a clear sense of what's right and what's wrong, you will have no trouble letting your conscience be your guide.

3.5 (continued)

" Be cheerful also, and seek not
external help nor the tranquillity
which others give.
A man then must stand erect,
not be kept erect by others. "

Be happy, and don't depend on the help or tranquillity that other people might give. Don't be reliant on their support; stand on your own two feet.

3.7

" Never value anything as profitable
to yourself which shall compel
you to break your promise, to lose
your self-respect, to hate any man,
to suspect, to curse, to act the
hypocrite, to desire anything which
needs walls and curtains. "

NEVER WANT SOMETHING that, in order to get it, you'd have to:

- break a promise

- lose your self-respect

- hate, wish misfortune on or be suspicious of others

- be hypocritical

- feel the need to hide something or keep a secret.

It might be tempting to transgress your values and principles, but it's not worth compromising yourself – that is, doing something that means you let yourself down.

So, what should you do instead?

Let go of what you covet and instead shift your focus to what you can achieve by fair and honest means.

3.9

" Reverence the faculty which produces opinion […] This faculty promises freedom from hasty judgement, and friendship towards men. "

=====

APPRECIATE YOUR ABILITY to rationalize and reason. Being able to calmly think things through helps you avoid acting in haste and regretting it later. This helps you to be considerate and thoughtful towards other people and thereby foster positive relationships.

Of course, our ability to think calmly can get away from us – our brains often get hijacked by our emotions and we react to situations and people in ways that don't always serve us – or others – well.

Most situations need clear, calm thinking rather than blind, emotional reaction. In a range of situations, you need to stop and think; to access the rational thinking part of your brain.

Emotions say hurry. Wisdom says wait.

Have faith in your ability to respond in a conscious, purposeful way, rather than react automatically.

3.10

" [B]ear in mind that every man
lives only this present time, which
is an indivisible point, and that all
the rest of his life is either past or
it is uncertain. "

We LIVE ONLY in the present; the rest of our life is either in the past or in an uncertain future.

Too often, we don't experience what's happening now because we're thinking about what did or didn't happen yesterday, last week and last month, or about what still needs doing or might happen tomorrow.

We can get stuck in the past, going back over events or paralysed by worries about the future. We let the present slip away and miss what's happening in the only moment that really exists – the present.

So, to bring your awareness to the present more often, set yourself an intention: each day, set aside a short amount of time when you do something devoted to being in the present. It could be something creative – cooking, drawing, mending or fixing something. Eating a meal, drinking a cup of tea, listening to a piece of music. Whatever you choose to do, just do that one thing. Give it your full attention.

3.14

" No longer wander at hazard;
hasten then to the end which
you have before you, and,
throwing away idle hopes,
come to your own aid, if you care
at all for yourself, while it is in
your power. "

STOP FAFFING AROUND; just get on with it. Stop hoping things will just happen. If you care about yourself, get a grip and take control … while you still can.

BOOK FOUR

4.2

" Let no act be done without a
purpose, nor otherwise than
according to the perfect
principles of art. "

Don't act without purpose or without following your guiding principles.

When you act with purpose, you act with intention; you are clear about what, how and why you are doing something. You're persistent; you determine to keep going until you achieve what you set out to do.

Your guiding principles are the values that influence your decisions – what you say and do.

For example, if honesty is important to you – that is, it is one of your values – being honest would be the guiding principle that influenced what you would or wouldn't do in every situation.

4.3

" [T]hings do not touch the soul,
for they are external and remain
immovable; but our perturbations
come only from the opinion
which is within. "

═══

THINGS HAPPEN OR they don't happen. Any distress that we feel about what does or doesn't happen comes from within ourselves.

According to what the Stoics called "the dichotomy of control", there are things we can control and things we cannot control. You can't always control what happens to you. But you *can* control how you feel and respond to what happens. Your thoughts can dwell on the difficulties – the negative aspects – of a situation. Or you can acknowledge the difficulties and then focus on what is good about the situation or what good can come out of it – the positive aspects.

If you change the way you look at things, the things you look at change.

You have power over your mind – not outside events.

4.3 (continued)

**" For the whole earth is a point,
and how small a nook in it is
this your dwelling. "**

EARTH IS A small speck that humanity lives on, and you live only in a tiny corner of that planet.

The astronomer Carl Sagan reminds us that when looked at from afar the earth is simply a pale blue dot and that humans' anthropocentrism – our "imagined self-importance, the delusion that we have some privileged position in the Universe" – is challenged by this point of pale light.*

To see the "pale blue dot" and understand more about what Sagan is talking about, go to planetary.org/worlds/pale-blue-dot.

* Carl Sagan, *Pale Blue Dot: A Vision of the Human Future in Space* (New York: Random House, 1994).

4.7

" Take away your opinion, and then
there is taken away the complaint,
'I have been harmed.' Take away
the complaint, 'I have been
harmed,' and the harm is
taken away. „

IF YOU BELIEVE yourself to have been harmed, then you will suffer. Take away the belief that you've been harmed and you will no longer suffer.

That's not to suggest that you ignore, deny or suppress problems, difficulties and pain. But know that, as another Stoic, Seneca, said, "A man is unhappy as he has convinced himself he is."*

And, as Shakespeare's Hamlet says, "there is nothing either good or bad, but thinking makes it so" (*Hamlet*, Act 2, Scene 2).

* Seneca, *Letters from a Stoic* (London: Penguin, 2004).

4.12

" [C]hange your opinion, if there is
any one at hand who sets you right
and moves you from any opinion.
But this change of opinion must
proceed only from a certain
persuasion, as of what is just or of
common advantage, and the like,
not because it appears pleasant or
brings reputation. "

CHANGE YOUR OPINION if someone else can show you that you are mistaken in your beliefs or can show good reason to think differently. But only change your opinion if a change of beliefs is guided by truth, reason, justice and fairness. Don't change your opinion because it sounds good or makes you look good.

4.18

" How much trouble he avoids
who does not look to see what his
neighbour says or does or thinks,
but only to what he does himself,
that it may be just and pure [...]
look not round at the depraved
morals of others, but run straight
along the line without deviating
from it. "

OF COURSE, OTHER people's thoughts, opinions and actions matter; they can influence and have an impact on you. But they should do so only up to a point.

If, for example, you are being criticized or maligned, you can choose how much you care about these criticisms and put-downs. They affect you only as much as you let them.

There is peace and calm to be had when you refuse to be overly affected by other people's opinions and actions. Choose to focus on what you can control – what *you* think and do.

4.20

" Everything which is in any way
beautiful is beautiful in itself [...]
Neither worse than nor better is a
thing made by being praised. [...]
Is such a thing as an emerald
made worse than it was, if it
is not praised? Or gold, ivory,
purple, a lyre, a little knife,
a flower, a shrub? "

EVERYTHING THAT IS beautiful is beautiful in itself. Praise doesn't make it any better or worse.

Is an emerald any less for not having been praised? Or gold, ivory, purple, a lyre, a little knife, a flower, a shrub?

They are all they need to be. Approval and admiration can't make things any more beautiful. Disdain and contempt can't spoil what is beautiful. As the famous line in *Romeo and Juliet* tells us: "A rose by any other name would smell as sweet" (Act 2, Scene 2).

4.22

" Do not be whirled about,
but in every movement have
respect to justice, and on the
occasion of every impression
maintain the faculty of
comprehension or
understanding. "

———

DON'T GET CONFUSED or wound up. Just be led by what is fair and aim to understand the situation or other person.

Take, for example, another driver overtaking you and speeding off, breaking the speed limit. Give them the benefit of the doubt: maybe they have something urgent – an emergency – to attend to. Railing about how inconsiderate and dangerous their behaviour was will just leave you feeling angry and resentful.

In a range of situations – a parent shouting at their child, someone jumping the queue, a dog owner allowing their dog off its leash – giving someone the benefit of the doubt is choosing to believe that they had good reason to behave as they did. When you don't know their circumstances, don't assume they had hostile intent.

Be curious rather than judgemental.

4.24

❝ [T]ranquillity […] comes from
doing well, but also […] from
doing few things. For the greatest
part of what we say and do being
unnecessary, if a man takes this
away, he will have more leisure
and less uneasiness. ❞

Only do what's essential. Do less, better. Because much of what we do or say is not essential. If you can eliminate it, you will experience more peace and calm.

What might be one thing you could stop doing? One thing that's not important or essential. One thing that, if you let it go, not only would you no longer have to do it, but also you'd no longer have to *think* about it.

Start today: eliminate something from your life; have more time and less stress.

4.31

“ Love the art, poor as it may be,
which you have learned,
and be content with it. „

Whatever your skills, however insignificant or unimportant you might think they are, reflect on them with pride – with self-respect and a sense of your personal worth.

What skills do you have? Think of some of the things you've learned to do – to cook, to drive, to use equipment or technology, to speak another language or to play a musical instrument.

Think of the time and energy you've spent learning to do these things. Feel good about yourself and give yourself credit for having learned to do these things; for having gone from little or no knowledge and ability to now being confident and capable.

4.43

" Time is like a river made up
of the events which happen,
and a violent stream; for as soon
as a thing has been seen, it is
carried away, and another comes
in its place, and this will be
carried away too. "

TIME IS LIKE a river of events. Once you have seen or experienced something, it is carried away, replaced by something else, which is also carried away.

All things will pass.

So, if you are currently experiencing a difficulty or a problem, remind yourself that it will eventually pass. And when life is good, reminding yourself that that too will pass encourages you to make the most of it. Be aware and appreciate your happiness before it passes by.

4.45

" In the series of things those which follow are always aptly fitted to those which have gone before; for this series is not like a mere enumeration of disjointed things, which has only a necessary sequence, but it is a rational connection: and as all existing things are arranged together harmoniously, so the things which come into existence exhibit no mere succession, but a certain wonderful relationship. "

WHAT FOLLOWS RELATES to what came before – not just as one thing follows another, but as an arrangement of parts, forming a consistent, rational whole.

In music, different sounds come together to create a wonderful, distinctive new sound – a harmony – and much the same happens in our lives, in nature and in the world.

4.49

" Be like the promontory against
which the waves continually break,
but it stands firm and tames the
fury of the water around it.

[…]

Remember too on every occasion
which leads you to vexation to
apply this principle; not that this
is a misfortune, but that to bear it
nobly is good fortune. "

STAND LIKE A rock against the breaking waves, firm and taming the fury of the water around you.

Remember, too, that when you are disturbed or distressed about something, rather than see it as misfortune, consider it your good fortune to have the dignity and bearing to withstand it.

BOOK FIVE

5.1

" Why then am I dissatisfied if
I am going to do the things for
which I exist and for which
I was brought into the world?
Or have I been made for this,
to lie in the bedclothes and keep
myself warm. "

WITH THESE WORDS, Marcus Aurelius is motivating himself to do his duty – what's expected of him. There's no reason for him to be discontent if he's starting the day with the aim of fulfilling his purpose. Were you, he chides himself, put on earth to lie in bed all day?

There might not be a lot to look forward to each morning – you'd rather stay in bed – but you've just got to get up and get on with it.

5.1 (continued)

" Do you not see the little plants,
the little birds, the ants, the spiders,
the bees working together to put
in order their several parts of the
universe? And are you unwilling
to do the work of a human being,
and do you not make haste to
do that which is according to
your nature? "

Everything in nature has a purpose – a purpose that benefits both the individual plant or animal and the ecosystem it belongs to. Every action aims towards preserving the balance and stability within the system.

It follows, then, that we humans, too, have a purpose – a reason to be here – that contributes to the rest of the world.

So, if everything else in nature is up doing what they're here for, you can, too. Step up and play your part!

5.3

" Judge every word and deed
which is according to nature to
be fit for you; and be not diverted
by the blame which follows from
any people, nor by their words,
but if a thing is good to be done
or said, do not consider it
unworthy of you. "

EVERYTHING YOU DO or say should be according to whether it is right for you – don't be influenced by other people who don't like what you say or do. If you believe it's right for you to say or do something, then go ahead.

5.6

" [A] man when he has done a
good act does not call out for
others to come and see, but he
goes on to another act, as a vine
goes on to produce again the
grapes in season. "

IF YOU DO someone a favour, there's no need to publicize it – to let everyone know about your good deed. Just like a vine produces grapes one season and then goes on to produce more grapes the next, having done one good deed, you simply move on to the next one.

A favour is something done or granted out of goodwill, not for recognition or remuneration. It's an act of kindness.

Remind yourself of the good that comes from a small act of kindness. This week, do someone a favour – a kindness. It doesn't have to be anything big – a small kindness that doesn't take too much effort is good. Here are some ideas:

- Do a chore that you don't normally do for someone else.

- Be thoughtful. Did your colleague have a bad day today? Bring them a coffee tomorrow morning.

- Buy someone – a colleague, neighbour, family or friend – a cake or some fresh fruit (for me, summer strawberries or raspberries are always welcome!).

- Offer to help deliver or collect something for someone.

5.9

" Be not disgusted, nor discouraged,
nor dissatisfied, if you do not
succeed in doing everything
according to right principles,
but when you have failed, return
back again, and be content if the
greater part of what you do is
consistent with man's nature. "

DON'T BE UPSET if you don't do everything right. If you make a mistake, or there are setbacks and difficulties, try again. Know that you have done your best.

Be pleased with what you did right and move forward with what you have learned from what went wrong. If you really want to achieve something, there's usually a way.

5.13

" I am composed of the formal and
the material; and neither of them
will perish into non-existence,
as neither of them came into
existence out of non-existence.
Every part of me then will be
reduced by change into some part
of the universe, and that again will
change into another part of the
universe, and so on for ever. "

LIKE MARCUS AURELIUS, everything that came before him and everything that came after him, we are part of the universe. Our physical self came from earth – from the universe – and our physical self will return to earth – to the universe.

Think about it: in one form or another, we have always existed *and* will exist for ever!

5.16

❝ Such as are your habitual
thoughts, such also will be the
character of your mind; for the
soul is dyed by the thoughts. ❞

IF YOU CONTINUALLY interpret events and experiences in the same ways, these become your habitual ways of thinking. Much like dying wool, our mind – our soul and spirit – is dyed by the thoughts we provide it.

This isn't just Stoic philosophizing. Science shows us that the more often we think in a certain way, the more likely we are to continue to think that way: it becomes our default way of thinking; it becomes a habit.

It's just like walking through a field of long grass: the more often that path is trodden, the more established the path becomes and the more likely it is that you'll take that path. It becomes automatic – a habit – and you don't have to think about it.

If, then, you often interpret events in an unhelpful, negative way, you establish negative thinking habits. However, if you get into a habit of thinking more positively about events, your mind will more likely continue to think in those ways.

Know, too, that the things you think about determine not only the quality of your mind but also the quality of your life.

You are what you think. And what you think, you are.

5.18

" Nothing happens to any man
which he is not formed by
nature to bear. **"**

Nothing happens to you that you can't manage. As a human being, you *do* have the ability to cope and withstand.

Rather than get yourself wound up and anxious about what might happen in a particular situation, make a plan:

- Identify what exactly it is that you're worried about. What's the worst that can happen?

- Identify your options: think what you can do to minimize or manage the worst-case scenario.

- Once you've decided which option to take, make a plan of action.

If you find yourself worrying, tell yourself, "Stop, I have a plan!" and keep your thoughts on that. Visualize a positive outcome: create images for yourself where you see yourself coping and things turning out OK.

5.20

" But so far as some men make
themselves obstacles to my proper
acts, man becomes to me one of
the things which are indifferent,
no less than the sun or wind or
a wild beast. Now it is true that
these may impede my action, but
they are no impediments to my
affects and disposition [...] for
the mind converts and changes
every hindrance to its activity
into an aid; and so that which is a
hindrance is made a furtherance
to an act; and that which is an
obstacle on the road helps us on
this road. "

PEOPLE, THINGS OR events might block your attempts to do something, but they can't block your good intentions.

If something gets in the way, it can give you pause to think what your options are, before you move forward.

What stands in the way becomes the way. There's always a way, and often there's more than one way. In a situation, for example, where someone is rude or offensive to you, you have the opportunity to practise a virtue – to be patient and tolerant.

The mind transforms obstacles into actions through the shaping of intentions. When faced with a hindrance, focus your mind to think creatively and come up with ideas, options and solutions.

5.29

" [I]t is in your power to live here.
But if men do not permit you, then
get away out of life, yet so as if you
were suffering no harm. The house
is smoky, and I quit it. "

You HAVE A right to be here. But if someone is stopping you, get away from them. If the house is full of smoke, get out.

What Marcus Aurelius is saying here can relate to the concept of bullying and harassment.

If you're being bullied, abused or harassed, if you feel that there is little or nothing you can do about it, leave. Leave the job, the relationship or the social media account.

By leaving, you regain control; you take away the opportunity for the bully to behave like this towards you.

Are you concerned that, if you leave, you've let the bully "win"?

Rather than think in terms of one of you winning or losing, think about keeping yourself safe and sane. Know that, if you take control and walk away, you can manage to find a new job or somewhere to live or whatever it is that you're worried about losing. What you can't manage is the bully. So, refuse to allow your life to be wrecked, and get out!

5.35

" If this is neither my own badness,
nor an effect of my own badness,
and the common weal [good] is
not injured, why am I troubled
about it, and what is the harm to
the common weal? "

IF SOMETHING HAPPENS but you've not done anything wrong and no one has been harmed, what's the problem?

BOOK SIX

6.2

" Let it make no difference to you
whether you are cold or warm,
if you are doing your duty; and
whether you are drowsy or satisfied
with sleep; and whether ill-spoken
of or praised. "

WHATEVER DISCOMFORT YOU might experience, it doesn't matter as long as you're doing what is most important; what's expected or required of you; or whatever is your moral or legal obligation.

In other words, just do the right thing – the rest doesn't matter. But doing the right thing is not always easy. The rest often *does* matter!

Courage can help you. Courage is one of the Stoic four virtues. Courage gives you the ability to do something despite any doubt or fear, pain or discomfort you might feel. Courage isn't having no fear, it's strength in the face of pain and fear.

And often, that first step towards doing the right thing is a courageous one.

6.6

**" The best way of avenging
yourself is not to become like
the wrongdoer. "**

THE BEST WAY to get revenge is to refuse to behave like the person who has done you wrong.

When you recognize a wrongdoer, you also recognize wrongdoing – how not to behave. What not to do is clear: whatever the other person has done, don't stoop to their level. By choosing not to retaliate against the wrongdoer, you elevate yourself – *you* are the better person.

6.7

" Take pleasure in one thing and
rest in it, in passing from one
social act to another social act. **"**

Do one thing at a time. Enjoy being fully engaged with that one thing. Then move on to the next thing.

Whatever it is you're doing, give it your complete attention. Then move on to the next task or activity. Give that your full attention, too. Just focus on one thing at a time.

How often are you doing one thing but worrying about something else or thinking about everything else that needs doing? Forget about multi-tasking. Don't try to do two things at once. Do one thing, fully and completely, at a time.

6.10

" The universe is either a confusion,
and a mutual involution of things,
and a dispersion, or it is unity and
order and providence. If then it is
the former, why do I desire to
tarry in a fortuitous combination
of things and such a disorder? [...]
But if the other supposition is
true, I venerate, and I am firm,
and I trust in him who governs. "

THE UNIVERSE IS either total chaos or complete order, uni-
fied by the foreseeing care and guidance of God or nature.
If the universe is total chaos, why care about anything as
you'll eventually just disperse as part of it? But if the universe is ordered, then you can respect and trust in its govern-
ing forces.

6.16

" Will you not cease to value many
other things too? Then you will
be neither free, nor sufficient for
your own happiness, nor without
passion. For of necessity you must
be envious, jealous, and suspicious
of those who can take away those
things, and plot against those who
have that which is valued by you. "

THE MORE YOU value and are attached to your possessions, the more dependent you are on them for your happiness. You risk being jealous and suspicious of anyone who could take away these things. Your envy may prompt you to plot against other people who have what you want.

How can you avoid jealousy and envy and coveting what others have that you do not? By acknowledging, appreciating and being thankful for what you *do* have. At the same time, you should be aware that what you have could be gone at any time.

6.16 (continued)

❝ But to reverence and honour your own mind will make thee content with yourself, and in harmony with society, and in agreement with the gods, that is, praising all that they give and have ordered. ❞

IF YOU RESPECT and value your own mind – your thoughts, feelings, beliefs and opinions – you can be content with yourself, in harmony with others and the universe; pleased with all that you receive.

6.19

" If a thing is difficult to be
accomplished by yourself, do not
think that it is impossible for man:
but if anything is possible for man
and conformable to his nature,
think that this can be attained by
yourself too. "

═══

IF YOU FIND it hard to do something, that doesn't make it impossible for anyone to do.

If someone else can do it, so can you.

However, while it is true that many things are achievable through effort and perseverance, we need to acknowledge that not everyone starts from the same place or has the same skills, strengths, opportunities and advantages.

Comparing yourself to others can sometimes be misleading, as everyone's path to success is different.

6.47

" One thing here is worth a great
deal, to pass your life in truth
and justice, with a benevolent
disposition even to liars and
unjust men. ,,

ONE SHOULD, MARCUS suggests, have a kind, forgiving attitude to other people's wrongdoings, to their lies and unfairnesses.

That said, you don't have to accept the wrongdoings of other people and you need to know that your response to their wrongdoings affects your ability to right them. You can lash out in anger or get stuck in resentment and bitterness. Or you can attempt to understand and respond with fairness. You have a choice.

6.52

" It is in our power to have no
opinion about a thing, and not to
be disturbed in our soul; for things
themselves have no natural power
to form our judgements. "

THINGS IN THEMSELVES don't have the ability to make us think in certain ways; they have no inherent power to form our judgements.

Furthermore, you don't have to have an opinion on everything; you don't have to make an issue out of every event and situation. Things don't need to bother you. You can be impartial.

Of course, you're entitled to your own opinion. But that doesn't mean you have to have one. For one thing, you might not know enough about an issue to make a judgement.

What you give your attention to is important: be prudent and discriminate between what does and does not require your attention. You *can* scroll past!

6.53

" Accustom yourself to attend
carefully to what is said by another,
and as much as it is possible,
be in the speaker's mind. "

LISTEN CAREFULLY TO what someone is telling you. Have empathy.

How often do you really listen to what someone is saying? That is, pay close attention and aim to understand?

It's not difficult. When listening to someone telling you something, listen as if you are going to have to repeat back what they have said. Doing this will help you listen closely and concentrate on what they're saying.

And to have empathy, rather than relating only to the other person's *situation*, relate to their *emotions*, their feelings. Maybe, for example, they're anxious about flying. You might not be anxious about flying, but you do know what it's like to feel anxious.

6.54

" That which is not good for
the swarm, neither is it good
for the bee. "

MARCUS IS HERE emphasizing the fact that within our family, friendship groups, business or community we are all connected and dependent on one another. The image of the hive suggests that what is detrimental to the well-being of a group is also harmful to the individuals within that group.

This meditation prompts the further question: Is what's good for the individual person always good for the group?

Balancing the needs of the individual vis-à-vis the needs of society is at the heart of all liberal democratic politics.

BOOK SEVEN

7.5

" Is my understanding sufficient
for this or not? If it is sufficient,
I use it for the work as an
instrument given by the universal
nature. But if it is not sufficient,
then […] give way to him who is
able to do it better. "

Do you understand what you're doing? If so, carry on; use your understanding as something given to you to do good. But if you don't know what you're doing, pass the activity on to someone who has a better understanding and ability to do it.

Don't use up your time and energy doing tasks that others may have more knowledge about or ability to do.

Furthermore, if what you are attempting to do is for the benefit of others, remember that you're not the only one affected if you don't get help from someone more suited to the task.

Passing over a task to someone else who can do it better frees you up to do what you – and maybe only you – can do well.

7.6

" How many after being celebrated
by fame have been given up to
oblivion; and how many who have
celebrated the fame of others have
long been dead. "

NOT ONLY ARE many who were once famous now unknown, but also those who gave them their fame have likewise been forgotten.

This was as true in Marcus's times as it is in ours. The proverbial "fifteen minutes of fame" means that the window of fame is short lived. A person's fame soon fades and is replaced by someone else's fame – a "celebrity" – whose actual abilities and achievements may or may not be limited, but whose visibility – for a short time – is extensive.

7.7

" Be not ashamed to be helped;
for it is your business to do your
duty like a soldier in the assault
on a town. How then, if being
lame you can not mount up on the
battlements alone, but with the
help of another it is possible? "

DON'T BE ASHAMED to get help. Like a soldier who is injured, how can you scale the battlements except with the help of another?

Do you ask for help when you don't know how to do something or you can't cope with what needs doing? Or do you just struggle through it?

Perhaps you think asking for help is a sign of weakness; that by asking for help you're admitting that you lack knowledge, skill or experience to do something yourself. But asking for help doesn't mean you're inadequate; it simply means you need assistance with something specific for a specific amount of time.

Maybe you assume that, if you ask others for help, they'll say no. But other people are more willing to help than you might think. If you don't ask, though, the answer is already no!

7.8

" Let not future things disturb you,
for you will come to them, if it
shall be necessary, having with you
the same reason which now you
use for present things. "

Don't worry about the future, because, when it comes, you will manage with the same abilities you currently have.

When you're worried or anxious, you may feel that you have no control over what could happen – how events might turn out and whether you'll be able to cope if things do go wrong.

Worry drags you out of the present moment and into an unknown future, allowing unrelenting doubts and fears to overwhelm your mind and paralyse you.

Think of an event in the past where you coped but where, before the event happened, you were anxious and worried about it. When the time came – especially if you had already prepared and had a plan to mitigate the worst – you dealt with it with your "weapons of reason": good sense and courage. You can do so again.

═══

7.15

" Whatever anyone does or says,
I must be good; just as if the gold,
or the emerald, or the purple,
were always saying this. Whatever
anyone does or says, I must be
emerald and keep my colour. "

———

MARCUS BELIEVED IN being good, which for him meant following the Stoic four values of courage, moderation, wisdom and justice. Just as it is the nature of purple, gold and emerald to be their true colours, Marcus's true colour was to be good. This was important to him. No matter what anyone else said or did, he needed to remain true.

So how can you be emerald and keep your colour? By knowing what your true colours – what your values – are.

We all have values, but we each have different values. Maybe you've not given much thought to what your values are, but that doesn't mean you don't have any. Your values are what's important and worthwhile to you in the way that you live, work and relate to yourself and other people.

Maybe what's important to you is being honest, fair and understanding. Or being persistent and reliable. To help you identify what's important to you, type "list of personal values" into a search engine and reflect on those you find.

7.17

" *Eudaemonia* [happiness] is a good daemon, or a good thing. "

HAPPINESS *IS* A good thing!
Happiness is of two kinds:

- *hedonic* happiness, which is rooted in short-lived pleasures

- *eudaemonic* happiness, which is a long-term sense of well-being and fulfilment.

Hedonic happiness comes from the small pleasures – the little things that give us shots of joy – while eudaemonic happiness is concerned with the contentment that comes from having meaning and purpose in our lives and reaching our full potential.

Marcus and the Stoics believed that we are each responsible for our own *eudaemonia* – that we can each work out for ourselves what gives our life meaning and purpose and so make ourselves happy. The ability to be happy is within our power; we have the wherewithal to make ourselves happy.

7.18

" Is any man afraid of change?
Why what can take place without
change? […] [C]an you take a
bath unless the wood undergoes a
change? And can you be nourished,
unless the food undergoes a
change? And can anything else
that is useful be accomplished
without change? Do you not
see then that for yourself also
to change is just the same, and
equally necessary for the
universal nature? "

WHAT CAN HAPPEN without change? Can anything useful be achieved without change? Do you see that it's the same for you ... for all of us?

There are some things, like changes in the weather, that we accept are out of our control. But too often we resist change; we cling to the past and fear an uncertain future. We try to hold on to people, places and things and we struggle to let go.

You might not be able to control a particular change or stop it from happening, but you can control how you respond to change. Make yourself aware of the positive things, such as new opportunities, that change brings. Acknowledge and do what you can to prepare for the difficult aspects of a change. Then look for and focus on the positive aspects.

7.21

" Near is your forgetfulness of all
things; and near the forgetfulness
of you by all. "

You ARE CLOSE to forgetting everything and close to being forgotten.

Soon we will have forgotten everything, and everyone will forget us. And those yet to come will not be remembered by those who follow them.

Two to three generations after we've died, it's unlikely that anyone will ever think of us. But that's OK: accepting the inevitability of death encourages us to live well – more fully – now. The present is the only time that we have and the only time that matters.

7.25

" Nature which governs the whole
will soon change all things you see,
and out of their substance will
make other things, and again
other things from the substance
of them, in order that the world
may be ever new. "

NATURE GOVERNS ALL and will soon change all you see so it can make other things, and then, in turn, other things out of them, so the world is always new.

Everything changes. Summer turns to autumn, autumn to winter, and then spring arrives and everything is new again. Some change happens right before your eyes, while other changes happen so slowly that in your lifetime you won't be aware of them. Either way, change is ever present.

7.27

" Think not so much of what you
have not as of what you have:
but of the things which you have
select the best, and then reflect
how eagerly they would have been
sought, if you had them not. At
the same time, however, take care
that you do not through being
so pleased with them accustom
yourself to overvalue them, so as to
be disturbed if ever you should not
have them. "

RATHER THAN DWELL on what you don't have, appreciate the good things you do have. But at the same time, don't prize them so highly that you would be upset if you lost them.

What are some of the best things – possessions, people, experiences – you have in your life? Imagine how much you would long for those things if you didn't have them. But know, also, not to be so attached to them that you would be bereft without them.

═══

7.47

" Look round at the courses of the
stars, as if you were going along
with them; and constantly consider
the changes of the elements into
one another. "

———

IMAGINE YOURSELF RUNNING with the stars and, at the same time, be aware of how everything changes – spring turns to summer, autumn to winter. The clouds move on, and the sun appears.

Take time to look for and appreciate instances of the beauty of nature, and recognize that you are a part of that.

Watch the stars and see yourself running with them.

What do you find to be beautiful? Which sights and sounds? Write a list of the things, the events and experiences you find beautiful. Keep your list handy and add to it instances of beauty as and when you come across them.

7.49

" Consider the past […] You may foresee also the things which will be. For they will certainly be of like form, and it is not possible that they should deviate from the order of the things which take place now; accordingly to have contemplated human life for forty years is the same as to have contemplated it for ten thousand years. For what more will you see? "

By considering the past you can predict what will happen. The future will be similar to the past and will be no different from the way things happen now. So, to think about human life for 40 years is the same as to think about it for ten thousand years. What more is there to know?

7.56

" Consider yourself to be dead,
and to have completed your life
up to the present time; and live
according to nature the remainder
which is allowed you. "

CONSIDER YOURSELF TO have died and to have come back to life to live a good, virtuous life.

Whatever has happened, whatever you've done in the past, let it go. The past is dead and gone. Start again. Start again with what is known in mindfulness practice as a "beginner's mind". Having a beginner's mind simply means that you engage with yourself, other people, events, objects and activities as if for the first time.

Let go of past wrongdoings and mistakes, beliefs, judgements and conclusions, and begin again with a fresh new approach and perspective. As a quotation attributed to the 19th-century novelist George Eliot says: "It's never too late to be what you might have been."

7.59

" Look within. Within is the
fountain of good, and it will ever
bubble up, if you will ever dig. „

THERE IS GOOD within you. It will always come to the surface, you just need to dig for it.

Not sure what's the right thing to do? Then dig deep and ask yourself some questions:

- What are your options?

- What might be the outcome of each option?

- What are the pros and cons of each option?

- How will what you do affect you and other people?

- Can you take responsibility for what happens if things don't turn out well?

But most importantly:

- What are your conscience and your intuition telling you is the right, good thing to do?

BOOK EIGHT

8.4

" [Consider] that men will do the
same things nevertheless, even
though you should burst. "

REALIZE THAT PEOPLE will still do things that you have little or no control over, no matter how wound up or angry you become.

8.8

" You have not leisure [or ability]
to read. But you have leisure
[or ability] to check arrogance:
you have leisure to be superior to
pleasure and pain: you have leisure
to be superior to love of fame,
and not to be vexed at stupid and
ungrateful people, nay even to care
for them. "

You MAY NOT have the time or ability to read, but you do have the time to check your arrogance and to be superior to pleasure and pain. You have the time to avoid the love of fame and to not be angered at stupid and ungrateful people, or even to care for them.

══

8.9

" Let no man any longer hear you
finding fault with the court life or
with your own. "

———

Don't let anyone hear you complaining about your privilege.

To one extent or another, most of us in the developed world are privileged – we have access to and enjoy things that many other people across the world do not. Perhaps you have running water, are securely housed, had an education, or have access to good health care. Maybe you have friends and family. Perhaps you have a job, own a car and go on holiday.

Of course, privilege is relative: what one person experiences as a privilege, someone else might think of as a right. But whenever you hear yourself complaining about any of these things, check your privilege!

8.10

" Repentance is a kind of self-
reproof for having neglected
something useful; but that which
is good must be something useful,
and the perfect good man should
look after it. "

REPENTANCE IS BERATING yourself for not having done something of use. If something is good, it is useful and so a good person should look after it.

8.16

" Remember that to change your
opinion and to follow him who
corrects your error is as consistent
with freedom as it is to persist in
your error. For it is your own, the
activity which is exerted according
to your own movement and
judgement, and indeed according
to your own understanding too. "

To CHANGE YOUR opinion because someone has pointed out the errors in your thinking is just as valid as persisting with your mistaken beliefs. You are free to make your own mistakes. So is everyone else.

As the Indian activist and politician Mahatma Gandhi pointed out: "Freedom to make mistakes is what gives freedom its value."

8.29

" Wipe out your imaginations by
often saying to yourself:
Now it is in my power to let no
badness be in this soul, nor desire,
nor any perturbation at all; but
looking at all things I see what
is their nature, and I use each
according to its value. "

TELL YOURSELF OFTEN: it's in my power not to do wrong or be bad, not to have wants or allow myself to be upset. I can see good in all things, according to their nature and worth.

Look for the good in everything and look for the best in other people. Think of something or someone who irritates or annoys you. Now think of one good thing about them. There will be something good!

8.32

❝ Well, but by acquiescing in the hindrance and by being content to transfer your efforts to that which is allowed, another opportunity of action is immediately put before you in place of that which was hindered. ❞

By ACCEPTING A hindrance and being OK with switching your efforts to what *can* be done, a new path immediately opens up.

With acceptance comes the understanding that sometimes there are blocks and obstacles that can't be removed. What could be more futile than resisting what already is? Don't waste too much time being angry or upset. Use your time more wisely: accept that this way is blocked, focus your time and energy more productively, and move on in a new direction.

8.33

" Receive [wealth or prosperity]
without arrogance; and be ready
to let it go. "

Whatever you are given and whatever you receive – wealth, prosperity, good health, happiness and so on – do so humbly and be ready to let it go.

Appreciate the value of what you have but without a sense of entitlement. Use what you have for the best. Be aware that at any moment you may no longer have it – it's not yours to keep.

8.47

" And even if you are pained
because you are not doing some
particular thing which seems to
you to be right, why do you not
rather act than complain? "

IF YOU'RE FEELING bad because you're not doing something you should, rather than complain, why don't you get on with doing the right thing?

Certainly, it's not always easy to motivate yourself to do something you know you should be doing. Instead of berating yourself, think of what you stand to gain from doing what you should. Just get started and keep your mind on the benefits – on what you stand to gain.

8.49

" Say nothing more to yourself than
what the first appearances report.
Suppose that it has been reported
to you that a certain person speaks
ill of you. This has been reported;
but that you have been injured,
that has not been reported. [...]
Thus then always abide by the
first appearances, and add nothing
yourself from within, and then
nothing happens to you. "

═══

THINK NOTHING MORE about what someone tells you. If you're told someone speaks ill of you, they didn't also tell you to be hurt and upset by that. By refusing to add upset and pain with your own thoughts and interpretations, you'll remain unharmed.

8.53

" Do you wish to be praised by
a man who curses himself thrice
every hour? Would you wish
to please a man who does not
please himself? "

Do you want praise from someone who thinks so little of themselves? Why try to please someone who doesn't please themselves?

8.56

" For though we are made
especially for the sake of one
another, still the ruling power
of each of us has its own office,
for otherwise my neighbour's
wickedness would be my harm,
which God has not willed,
in order that my unhappiness
may not depend on another. "

ALTHOUGH WE ARE made to support each other, still I can make my own decisions; otherwise someone else's wickedness could be a bad influence on me. God has not willed that my unhappiness is the result of another person's influence.

8.61

" Enter into every man's ruling
faculty; and also let every other
man enter into yours. "

TRY TO UNDERSTAND what's going on in someone else's mind. And let others understand what's going on in your mind by being truthful and transparent.

BOOK NINE

9.4

" He who does wrong does wrong
against himself. He who acts
unjustly acts unjustly to himself,
because he makes himself bad. "

To DO HARM is to do yourself harm. To do an injustice is to do yourself an injustice. It reduces you; it degrades you.

9.5

" He often acts unjustly who does
not do a certain thing; not only
he who does a certain thing. "

IT'S NOT JUST what you do, it's also what you don't do that's important. Maybe you believe that, as long as you're not actively participating in wrongdoing, you're not responsible for any injustice that may be happening.

But when you're aware of an injustice or wrongdoing, by failing to intercede, you contribute to and perpetuate that injustice. By saying or doing nothing, the distress and harm continue unchecked. Your inaction is just as harmful as if you had initiated the wrongdoing yourself.

Doing nothing enables injustice to persist. Of course, you can't put right all the wrongs in the world, but in your own world, when it is safe to do so, take a stand, speak up and speak out.

What injustice or unfairness – big or small – could you show your support for today?

9.13

" Today I have got out of all
trouble, or rather I have cast out
all trouble, for it was not outside,
but within and in my opinions. "

═══

ONCE AGAIN, MARCUS reminds himself that he has the power to avoid upset, difficulty and distress, simply by the way he interprets what does and doesn't happen.

9.14

" All things are the same,
familiar in experience, and
ephemeral in time, and worthless
in the matter. Everything now is
just as it was in the time of those
whom we have buried. "

ALL THINGS ARE the same and there's nothing new; everything is short-lived, transitory and of no importance. All is the same now as it was for those who are long gone.

What has been will be again; what has been done will be done again. Of course, there have been and will be inventions and innovations, but they don't amount to any fundamental change in nature and human nature, both of which have remained and will always remain the same.

9.17

" For the stone which has been
thrown up it is no evil to come
down, nor indeed any good to
have been carried up. "

JUST BECAUSE A stone is thrown up into the air doesn't mean it's any better when it comes down. It is still just a stone.

Too often, we look at a thing, a situation or experience and say that it's a good or bad thing for it to have happened. But it is still just a thing, a situation or an event.

This Taoist parable reflects the same message:

One day a farmer's horse escaped. His neighbours said, "Oh, that's too bad!" And he said, "Maybe."

The next day the horse came back and brought seven wild horses with it. All the neighbours said, "Well, that's great, isn't it?" And the farmer said, "Maybe."

The following day, as his son was out riding one of the horses, he fell off and broke his leg. The neighbours said, "Well, that's too bad, isn't it?" And the farmer said, "Maybe."

The next day the conscription officers came to recruit men into the army. They rejected the farmer's son because he had a broken leg. Everyone said, "That's great, isn't it?" and the farmer said, "Maybe."

So, it's not possible to tell whether something that happens is good or bad. It's just a thing, an event or situation.

9.27

❝ When another blames you or hates you, or when men say about you anything injurious, approach their poor souls, penetrate within, and see what kind of men they are. You will discover that there is no reason to take any trouble that these men may have this or that opinion about you. However, you must be well disposed towards them, for by nature they are friends. ❞

WHEN SOMEONE BLAMES or hates you, or says something harmful, look at what kind of person they are. You will learn that there's no reason to be concerned about what they think about you. Respond with goodwill; just like you, they are human.

If someone blames you, they may be avoiding taking responsibility themselves. If they hate you, they may have fear in their hearts. If they say slanderous things about you, they may be jealous of you.

With an open mind, try to understand their motivations. Just like you, they may be struggling.

9.35

❝ Loss is nothing else than change.
But the universal nature delights
in change. ❞

LOSS BRINGS PAIN and sorrow. One minute you have something, then it's gone.

Whatever the loss – a loved one, a job, your home, money or a possession – you're left feeling upset and bereft, maybe even devastated.

Marcus suggests that, although loss can bring pain and sorrow, as is inherent in nature, loss and change hold the potential for new beginnings. Understanding this can help us to manage loss with acceptance. Of course, that won't happen immediately – it takes time to adjust – but once we have accepted and adjusted, loss can be a catalyst for change and positive personal transformation.

9.42

❝ Consider whether you should not rather blame
yourself, because you did not expect such a man to
err in such a way. For you had means given you by
your reason to suppose that it was likely that he
would commit this error, and yet you have forgotten
and are amazed that he has erred.

But most of all when you blame a man as faithless
or ungrateful, turn to yourself. For the fault is
manifestly your own, whether you did trust that
a man who had such a disposition would keep his
promise, or when conferring your kindness you did not
confer it absolutely, nor yet in such a way as to have
received from your very act all the profit. For what
more do you want when you have done a man a service?
Are you not content that you have done something
conformable to your nature, and do you seek to be paid
for it? Just as if the eye demanded a recompense for
seeing, or the feet for walking. ❞

THINK ABOUT IT: if someone has let you down or done you wrong in some way, why would you be amazed if they behave that way again?

When you blame a person for being disloyal or ungrateful, turn to yourself. You are the one at fault. Whether you trusted someone who you already knew would not keep their promise, or when doing them a kindness you expected something in return, aren't you satisfied with having done good or do you seek payment? Just as if the eye expected compensation for seeing or the feet to be paid for walking.

BOOK TEN

10.3

" Remember […] you are formed
by nature to bear everything,
with respect to which it depends
on your own opinion to make
it endurable and tolerable, by
thinking that it is either your
interest or your duty to do this. "

You ARE BORN with the ability to bear everything, either because you recognize it to be in your interest or because it is your duty to do so.

Despite what Marcus says here, we may *not* have the ability to bear everything – high levels of stress and trauma can overwhelm each and any one of us. However, to a large extent, our ability to cope is in our control: we each have the ability to deal with most situations, cope with difficulties and challenges, and bounce back. This ability is called resilience.

There are several factors that contribute towards resilience: for example realistic expectations, confidence in your abilities to cope, the ability to look for the positive, and an ability to seek and accept help and support from other people.

10.12

“ What need is there of suspicious
fear, since it is in your power to
inquire what ought to be done?
And if you see clear, go by this way
content, without turning back; but
if you do not see clear, stop and
take the best advisers. ”

IF YOU ARE clear about what to do, go ahead and without turning back. If you're unsure, stop and take the best advice. There's nothing to fear either way.

There's nothing commendable in continuing to struggle with something. There's always someone – a friend, a family member, a neighbour or colleague – who can give you their opinion or recommendation. And these days, if none of those people is available, there's always a support group or an online community that can help and advise you.

10.16

" No longer talk at all about the
kind of man that a good man
ought to be, but be such. "

IT'S EASY TO get caught up in criticizing other people's actions and arguing about what is the good and the bad way to behave.

The concept of the "Circles of Influence", developed by the writer Stephen Covey, is helpful here.* There are three circles: the Circle of Concern is the wide range of concerns – the behaviour of celebrities and politicians, for example – which we condemn but over which we have little or no control. The Circle of Influence involves the concerns we can do something about. We may not always have control over their outcome but we can influence it with what we can control. The Circle of Control is what we can directly control or impact – through our own thoughts, words and actions.

Two thousand years earlier, Marcus was telling himself much the same thing: not to be overly concerned with the actions of other people, whether they are good or bad. Instead, focus on being a good person yourself.

* Stephen Covey, *The 7 Habits of Highly Effective People*, reissue edition (New York: Simon & Schuster, 2013).

10.30

" When you are offended at any
man's fault, forthwith turn to
yourself and reflect in what like
manner you err yourself. [...]
For by attending to this you will
quickly forget your anger, if this
consideration also is added. "

THINK OF A time when you were offended – annoyed or upset – by something someone else said or did. Have you ever behaved in the same way and offended someone? It's not always easy to see, but suppose, for example, you are annoyed with a friend because they rarely turn up on time to meet you. What is it about their poor punctuality that bothers you? Is it their lack of consideration? Most likely, you've been inconsiderate of other people, too. This doesn't excuse the other person, but reflecting on your own misdemeanours can help you manage the situation more calmly.

10.31

❝ Persevere then […] as the
blazing fire makes flame and
brightness out of everything
that is thrown into it. ❞

BE A BLAZING fire. Whatever is thrown at you, turn it into something positive, full of warmth and light.

BOOK ELEVEN

11.1

" These are the properties of the
rational soul: it sees itself, analyses
itself, and makes itself such as it
chooses; the fruit which it bears
itself enjoys — for the fruits of
plants and that in animals which
corresponds to fruits others enjoy. "

A REASONABLE PERSON is self-aware, observes and analyses themselves, creates themselves and reaps the rewards. By contrast, the fruits of plants and produce of animals are for others to enjoy.

11.4

" Have I done something for the
general interest? Well then, I have
had my reward. Let this always be
present to your mind, and never
stop [doing such good]. "

HAVE YOU DONE something that benefits others? That in itself is your reward. Keep this in mind and continue to do good.

11.7

" How plain does it appear that there is not another condition of life so well suited for philosophizing as this in which you now happen to be. "

IT'S CLEAR THAT *now* is the time to think about matters of philosophy: the nature of knowledge, for example, the meaning of life, the concepts of authenticity, free will, justice, courage, patience and virtue. All these issues are universal and eternal, and right now, you are experiencing them. So, think about them; explore and challenge your ideas and beliefs about life.

11.15

" The man who is honest and good
ought to be exactly like a man who
smells strong, so that the bystander
as soon as he comes near him must
smell whether he choose or not. "

THERE'S NO NEED to announce you are honest and good: it will be clear from your behaviour. It's the same as if you had a strong smell about you: you wouldn't have to proclaim it since it would be obvious as soon as anyone came near.

11.15 (continued)

" Nothing is more disgraceful
than a wolfish friendship
[false friendship].
Avoid this most of all. „

IT's SHAMEFUL TO be a false friend. Avoid it.

What's a false friend? It's someone who can't be trusted, is unreliable and disrespectful. A false friend could be someone who is unsupportive, or who takes more from the friendship than they give.

Avoid being a false friend. And avoid having false friends.

11.17

" Consider whence each thing is
come, and of what it consists, and
into what it changes, and what
kind of a thing it will be when
it has changed, and that it will
sustain no harm. "

THINK BEFORE YOU do something and what your motivation is – might your actions create changes that will result in harm? Whatever you intend to do, if it's not right, don't do it. If it's not true, don't say it.

Keep in mind this piece of advice. Before you speak, let your words pass through three gates: at the first gate, ask yourself, "Is it true?" At the second gate ask, "Is it necessary?" At the third gate ask, "Is it kind?" If it can't pass through at least two gates, it's better left unsaid.

11.18

" [C]onsider that you do not even understand whether men are doing wrong or not, for many things are done with a certain reference to circumstances. And in short, a man must learn a great deal to enable him to pass a correct judgement on another man's acts. "

IT'S NOT ALWAYS clear whether someone else is doing something wrong; so often their behaviour needs to be seen in relation to their circumstances. We must know a lot more before we criticize and judge what someone else is doing.

If, for example, you saw someone shoplifting a loaf of bread, they would be stealing and that's wrong. But what do you know of their circumstances – the reason they stole the bread? It's easy to jump to conclusions about someone else's behaviour without fully knowing the full picture. Rather than judge, be curious.

11.18 (continued)

" Consider that you also do many
things wrong, and that you are a
man like others; and even if you
do abstain from certain faults,
still you have the disposition
to commit them, though either
through cowardice, or concern
about reputation, or some such
mean motive. "

THINK ABOUT IT: although you do wrong, just like everyone else, you're human. Even if you do refrain from wrongdoing, you're still human: you may still do wrong because you are afraid, concerned about your reputation, or for some other personal reason.

11.18 (continued)

❝ How much more pain is brought
on us by the anger and vexation
caused by such acts than by the
acts themselves. ❞

How MUCH MORE harmful are the consequences of anger than the causes of it.

Something happens. It makes you angry. But whatever has happened, it's your reaction to it that upsets you – not what happened. Reacting with anger causes more damage than the action itself.

11.18 (continued)

" [T]o expect bad men not to
do wrong is madness, for he
who expects this desires an
impossibility. "

IT IS MAD to expect that bad people will stop doing bad things. People do reveal their true nature through their actions and behaviour. As the writer Maya Angelou has said: "When someone shows you who they are, believe them the first time."

BOOK TWELVE

12.1

" All those things at which you wish to arrive by a circuitous road you can have now, if you do not refuse them to yourself. And this means, if you will take no notice of all the past, and trust the future to providence, and direct the present only conformably to piety and justice. "

EVERYTHING YOU WISH for is attainable right now, but you're going about things in a roundabout way.

Forget about what's happened in the past, stop procrastinating, trust in God and nature, and just be truthful and respectful.

12.1 (continued)

❝ If then, whatever the time may
be when you shall be near to your
departure […] and if you shall be
afraid not because you must some
time cease to live, but if you shall
fear never to have begun to live
according to nature – then you will
be a man worthy of the universe
which has produced you. ❞

MARCUS IS NOT at his clearest here, but this is my interpretation: it is far better to fear death because it will be the end of your life than to fear death because you have not fully lived.

12.15

" Does the light of the lamp shine
without losing its splendour until
it is extinguished? And shall the
truth which is in you and justice
and temperance be extinguished
[before your death]? "

JUST AS A lamp continues to shine light until it is extinguished, each of us has a light within which shines out honesty, fairness, moderation and self-control. As long as you are alive, keep your light shining.

12.20

" First, do nothing inconsiderately,
nor without a purpose. Second,
make your acts refer to nothing
else than to a social end. "

DON'T DO ANYTHING without having a good reason and an aim – an intended result. And don't do anything without a thought or care for the rights or feelings of others. Be sure that what you do is of benefit to others.

12.24

" [W]ith respect to what may
happen to you from without,
consider that it happens either by
chance or according to providence,
and you must neither blame
chance nor accuse providence. "

WHATEVER HAPPENS TO you, it is either random – without a definite reason – or it is predestined – for a particular reason or purpose. Whatever the cause, don't look to lay blame. Accept it. It is what it is.

12.28

" To those who ask, Where have
you seen the gods, or how do you
comprehend that they exist and
so worship them, I answer, in the
first place, they may be seen even
with the eyes; in the second place,
neither have I seen even my own
soul, and yet I honour it. Thus
then with respect to the gods,
from what I constantly experience
of their power, from this
I comprehend that they exist,
and I venerate them. "

To anyone who asks me where I've seen the gods and how I even know they exist, my answer is that I can see them in their actions – in the beauty and power of nature. Similarly, I can't see my own mind, but I know it's there and what it can do.

12.29

" The safety of life is this, to examine everything all through, what it is itself, that is its material, what the formal part; with all your soul to do justice and to say the truth. What remains, except to enjoy life by joining one good thing to another so as not to leave even the smallest intervals between? "

To BE OF sound mind involves being aware of things: the basic, invariable nature of each thing; its significant individual feature; the form or pattern that governs a particular thing, or the genus to which it belongs. You must also be fair, honest and truthful. What remains, except to enjoy life, filling it with good, enjoyable things?

Also available as part of the Timeless Wisdom series

AUTOBIOGRAPHY
OF A YOGI
Paramahansa
Yogananda

Autobiography of a Yogi: Timeless Wisdom Distilled by
Paramahansa Yogananda

Embark on a journey of spiritual discovery and inner transformation.

In his extraordinary *Autobiography of a Yogi*, Paramahansa
Yogananda shares a visionary account of his life, teachings and
encounters with saints, sages and seekers. A gateway into India's
spiritual heritage, it is one of the most influential memoirs of
the 20th century.

This distilled edition features the most powerful teachings from
the original text, accompanied by illuminating commentary from
bestselling author Gill Hasson. Deeply inspiring and accessible,
it invites you to explore a life of purpose, connection and
self-realization.

Hardback ISBN: 978 1 399 82152 0
Ebook ISBN: 978 1 399 82153 7

For more information, please visit www.johnmurraypress.co.uk

Also available as part of the Timeless Wisdom series

THE PROPHET

Kahlil Gibran

The Prophet: Timeless Wisdom Distilled by Kahlil Gibran

Let poetry open the door to wisdom, beauty and inner peace.

Kahlil Gibran's *The Prophet* is a luminous meditation on love,
freedom, sorrow and joy. These poetic essays capture life's deepest
truths with grace and simplicity, sharing timeless insight into the
human spirit.

This distilled edition brings together the most enduring passages,
supported by thoughtful reflections from bestselling author
Gill Hasson. A soul-stirring companion for reflection, it's a book
to return to again and again for guidance and inspiration.

Hardback ISBN: 978 1 399 82154 4
Ebook ISBN: 978 1 399 82155 1

For more information, please visit www.johnmurraypress.co.uk

Also available as part of the Timeless Wisdom series

THINK AND
GROW RICH

Napoleon Hill

Think and Grow Rich: Timeless Wisdom Distilled by Napoleon Hill

Discover the power of your thoughts to shape your destiny.

Think and Grow Rich is Napoleon Hill's timeless guide to achieving
personal and financial success. Drawing on the insights of history's
most successful figures, it sets out a practical blueprint for turning
desire into achievement through belief, persistence
and focused thought.

This distilled edition features all of the original's most powerful
lessons, paired with fresh and revealing commentary from
bestselling author Gill Hasson. Clear, compelling and deeply
relevant today, it's your essential guide to unlocking your
potential and creating the life you want.

Hardback ISBN: 978 1 473 63626 2
Ebook ISBN: 978 1 473 63627 9

For more information, please visit www.johnmurraypress.co.uk

RAISING READERS
Books Build Bright Futures

Dear Reader,

We'd love your attention for one more page to tell you about the crisis in children's reading, and what we can all do.

Studies have shown that reading for fun is the **single biggest predictor of a child's future life chances** – more than family circumstance, parents' educational background or income. It improves academic results, mental health, wealth, communication skills, ambition and happiness.[1]

The number of children reading for fun is in rapid decline. Young people have a lot of competition for their time. In 2024, 1 in 10 children and young people in the UK aged 5 to 18 did not own a single book at home.[2]

Hachette works extensively with schools, libraries and literacy charities, but here are some ways we can all raise more readers:

- Reading to children for just 10 minutes a day makes a difference
- Don't give up if children aren't regular readers – there will be books for them!
- Visit bookshops and libraries to get recommendations
- Encourage them to listen to audiobooks
- Support school libraries
- Give books as gifts

There's a lot more information about how to encourage children to read on our website: **www.RaisingReaders.co.uk**

Thank you for reading.

hachette
UK

[1] National Literacy Trust, Book Ownership in 2024, November 2024
https://nlt.cdn.ngo/media/documents/Book_ownership_in_2024

[2] OECD. 2021. 21st-century readers: developing literacy skills in a digital world. Paris, France: OECD Publishing.
https://www.oecd.org/en/publications/21st-century-readers_a83d84cb-en.html